wisdom
and wonder

wisdom
and wonder

a collection of quotes
on love, hope and life

collected and illustrated
by kylie johnson

hardie grant books

for
mum who gave me a paintbrush,
and dad who gave me a pen ...

and
for my beloved oma
myrtle
whose words of wisdom and humour will be forever treasured,
who gave me the first quote i knew by heart
and live by to this day ...

foreword

'Love many, trust few, always paddle your own canoe' was written in my autograph book in the late seventies by my grandmother Myrtle. No other words but these few could better describe this woman, and every day I feel blessed to have inherited even a sliver of her love and tenacity. It was, as the dedication to this book says, the first 'quote' I remember knowing, understanding and being charmed by.

I was six and the small blue autograph book with a Holly Hobbie illustration on the cover became an object of reflection. The book is lost today (having maybe, or maybe not, survived family house fires, floods or general boxed-memory-accumulation). But the ink, her writing and its message are as clear to me today as they were then.

I never thought that I would be writing about my love of words so many years on. But, maybe even then, subconsciously, I was. And that is why I remember my grandmother's autograph so vividly. And this is why Myrtle deserves to be part of this book's dedication.

There is nothing new about quotes. They have been around in oral histories; as words scribed on walls and tablets; in holy books and teachings of science, art and philosophy; in novels and plays and poetry and songs. And at every turn now in the twenty-first century.

I was a child of the seventies and a teenager of the eighties. My generation is the last brought up *solely* as children and teenagers without the computer, the mobile phone and 'social media' where we communicate rapidly in small bites of words as a part of our daily routine.

Yet greeting cards with messages are still being made, school yearbooks signed, letters penned, songs written and sung, movie lines quoted. And, of course, luckily in this age, books are still being written, printed and read.

In some ways the computer age is enhancing all this. Quotes are being shared, liked and re-posted through the online hoopla. Don't get me wrong – it warms my heart and tickles my funny bone when a quote shows on my computer screen or phone most days. But I wonder sometimes how much wisdom is retained. Or does much of it turn into white noise? My hope is that the wisdom truly sticks, really sinks in and then, hopefully, is applied. I do wonder, though, if wisdom spread through social media inspires as much as the quiet essence of a handwritten note or words on the page of a book.

Well over ten years ago, I had, through circumstance, to divine a new creative world for myself. As with most parts of my life, I turned to words. After many years of having decorated clay pieces made by the hands of talented others, I began making my own ceramics and had to find my own creative way. This is where I combined words and clay in ways I hadn't explored previously. I put quotes I had collected for most of my life *into* the clay. So there I was moving words from paper pages into clay – earth to earth. And now with this book I have collected them back to paper – for you.

Over the past ten years I have made hundreds of

thousands of my signature ceramic 'quote tags' in my studio, paper boat press. These precious quotes, pressed into clay and fired, now live in homes all around the world – little collections of inspiration that are *of* the earth, spoken by some of its most inspired people. Words made permanent.

My philosophy when making the quote tags is that the words and what they say be universal. This approach, on reflection, was somehow conscious and is the way I wander through life. No matter your age, gender, background, heart, story – I hope the quotes speak to each of you, without exclusion.

Letters and emails arrive daily from people who have found the right quote to give and share, or to help themselves. These messages are often words of simple thanks, and they are fuel for my crazy artistic journey. However, the quotes are not mine and it is not me to be thanked. I am only the vessel who has shared the words, not the creator. And I never forget that.

Often when I cannot find the right words to say to a friend or loved one, or even to myself, I find that someone more eloquent has said just the right thing.

These men and women, famous or anonymous, from decades and centuries past, offer words of wisdom and truth. *That* is the magic of words.

Something experienced, felt and written about hundreds of years ago can still ring true. Truth is at the core of what it is to be human. We are all one. The same – flesh, blood and spirit – and not just now, but in all time.

It is often said that what is spoken or written today has more than likely already been thought of and said by someone before, just re-adjusted and spoken in a way that fits a generation, a century or an era.

One of my favourite quotes is from Isaac Newton: 'If I have seen further it is by standing on the shoulders of giants'. This illustrates on many levels what I mean. It is a centuries-old theory that we only know what we know now because of what has come before. The difference in applying it to a quote and spreading a simple thought is that it humbles us and makes us reflect. It not only links us to the message but makes us think (hopefully) that we are all connected by the progress of time. We must never forget that what has gone before has got us to this point in the human and earthly experience.

In this little book I have put together a small, yet insightful, collection of quotes. The blessing for me is that it has come to serve as a retrospective of the past ten years of quotes in clay. I look back and marvel that a small idea has taken so many turns. Maybe it is really the little six-year-old girl in me – the girl who could recite quotes – who is most excited by it all.

I hope you find some wisdom and wonder in these quotes that I have lived and loved by. I am truly grateful you hold this hyacinth.

kylie x

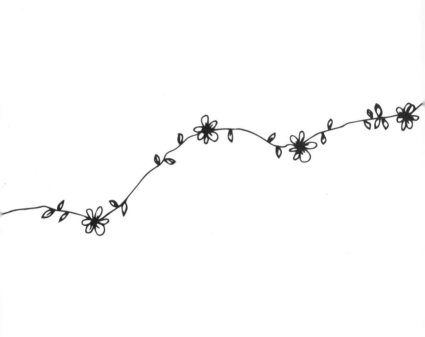

wisdom begins in wonder

socrates

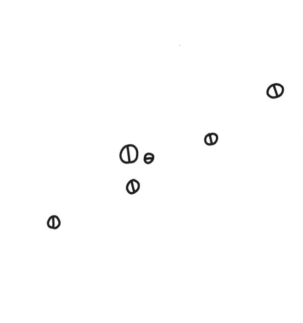

who so ever loves believes the impossible

elizabeth barrett browning

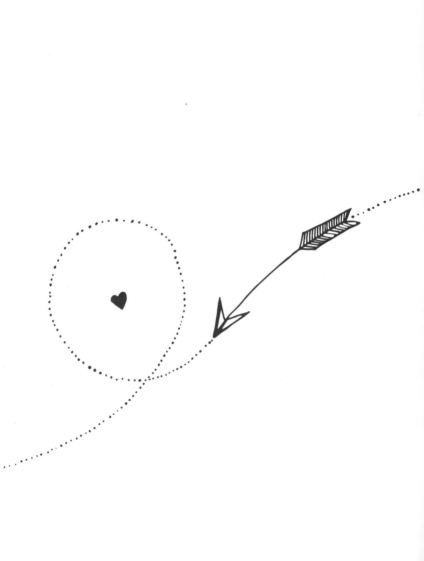

wherever you go

go
with
all
your
heart

confucius

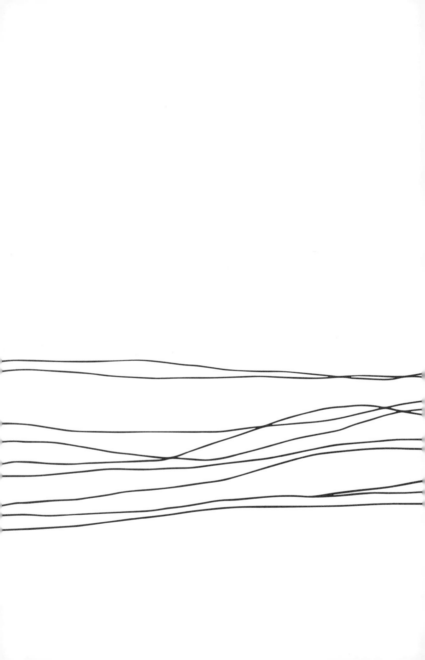

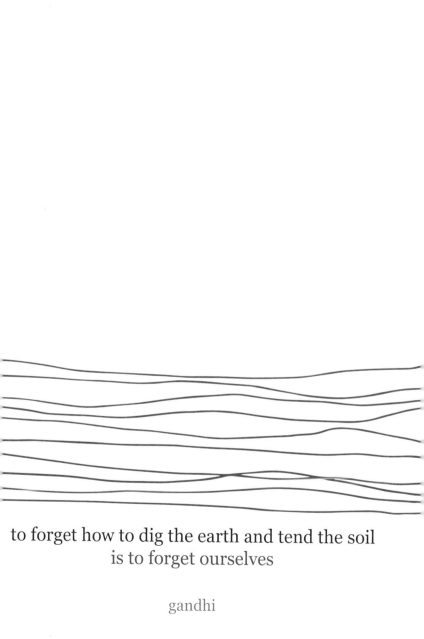

to forget how to dig the earth and tend the soil
is to forget ourselves

gandhi

the woods would be very silent

if no birds sang there
except those that sang best

henry van dyke

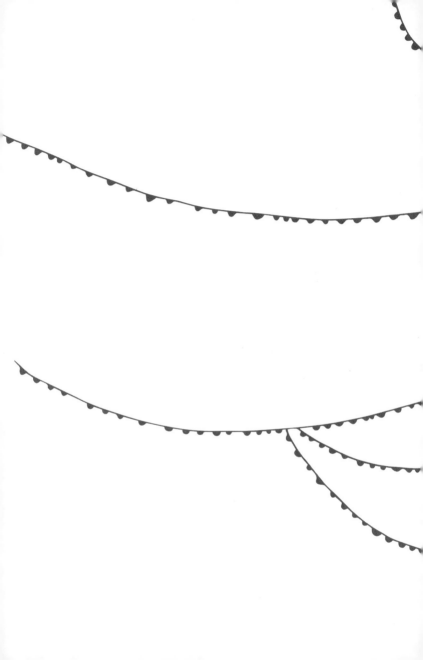

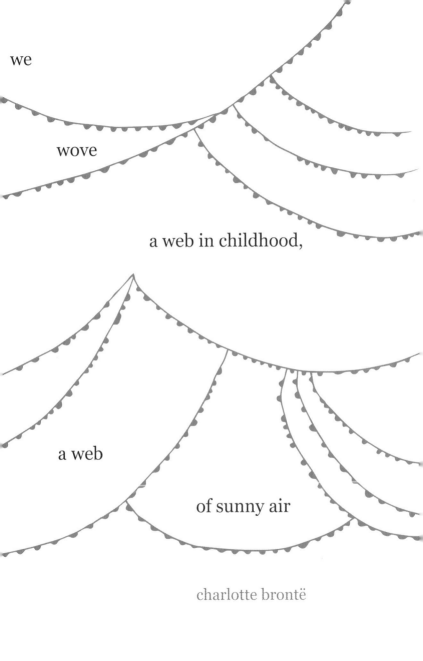

we

wove

a web in childhood,

a web

of sunny air

charlotte brontë

the creation of beautiful things
is the test of all great civilisations;

it is what makes

the life of each citizen

a sacrament

and not a speculation

oscar wilde

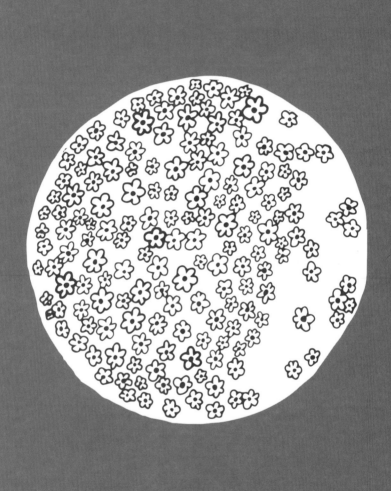

earth laughs in flowers

ralph waldo emerson

some books leave us free
some books make us free

ralph waldo emerson

where
thou
art,

that

is home

emily dickinson

the
soul would
have no rainbow
had the eyes no tears

john v cheney

rich in the simple worship of a day

john keats

i have loved the stars too fondly
to be fearful of the night

sarah williams

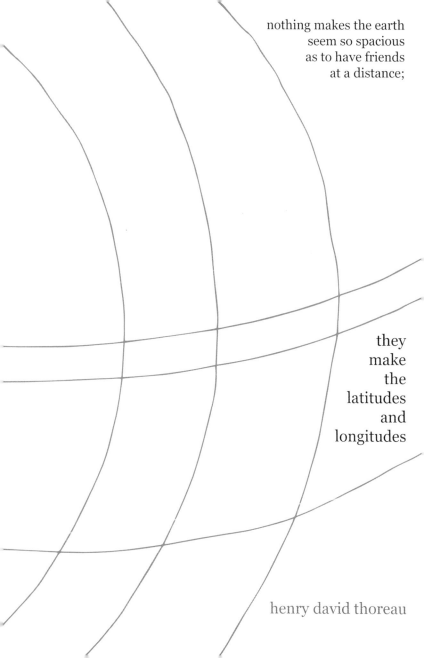

nothing makes the earth
seem so spacious
as to have friends
at a distance;

they
make
the
latitudes
and
longitudes

henry david thoreau

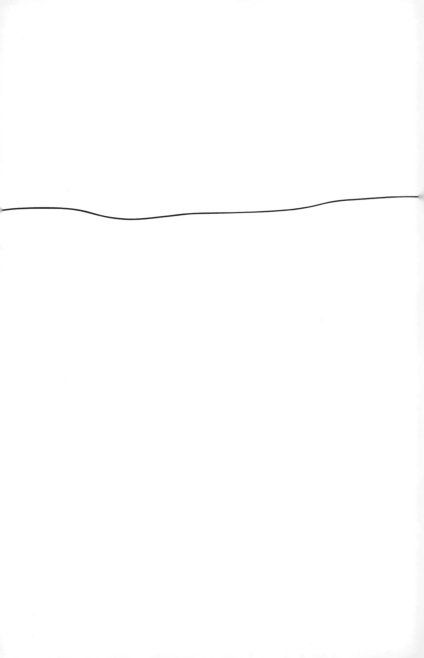

the love we give away

is the only love we keep

elbert hubbard

nothing
is worth more
than this day

goethe

we need

never

be ashamed of our tears

charles dickens

may your life be like a wildflower
growing freely in the beauty of each day

native american proverb

live

to

the

point

of

tears

albert camus

the measure of love

is to love

without measure

st francis de sales

may every sunrise
hold more promise,
and every sunset
hold more peace

blessing

life shrinks **or expands**
in proportion to one's courage

anaïs nin

it
takes
a village
to raise a child

african proverb

wine
is
sunlight
held
together
by
water

galileo

it is in the shelter of each other that people live

irish proverb

in the depth of winter i finally learned
that there was
in me

an invincible summer

albert camus

if you have a garden
and a library

you have
everything
you need

cicero

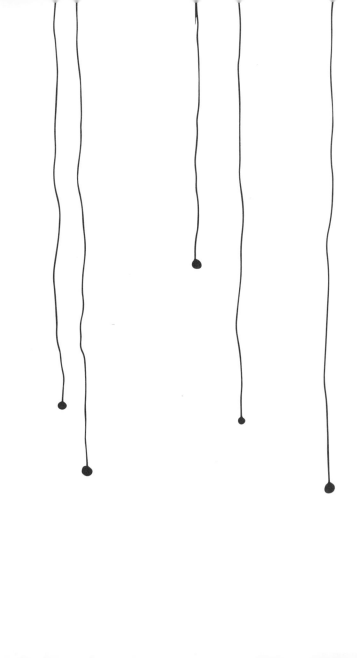

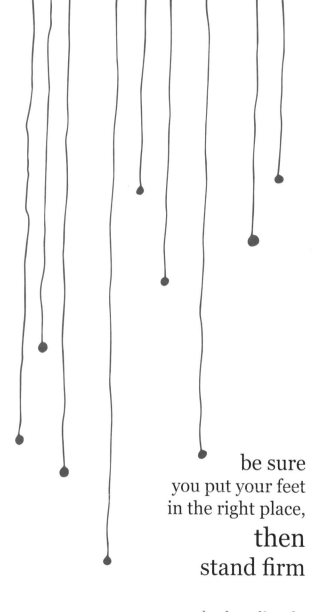

be sure
you put your feet
in the right place,
then
stand firm

abraham lincoln

i'll try out the pencils

sharpened to the point of infinity

which always sees

a h e a d

frida kahlo

the beautiful rests
on the foundations of the necessary

ralph waldo emerson

i invent **nothing,**
i rediscover

auguste rodin

i cook with wine,

sometimes

i even add it to the food

wc fields

love me when i least deserve it

because that is when i really need it

swedish proverb

the

years

teach

us

much

which

the

days

never

knew

ralph waldo emerson

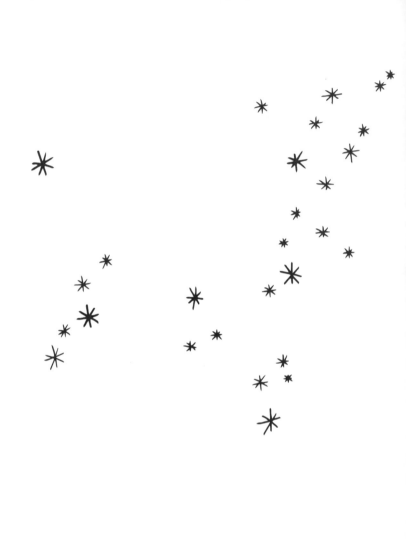

we are all in the gutter

but some of us

are looking at the stars

oscar wilde

where there is great love

there are always miracles

willa cather

whatever
our souls are made of

his and mine are the same

emily brontë

we do not
inherit
the world from
our ancestors,

we borrow it
from our children

native
american
proverb

we are but birds
of passage
and must build
our nests
out of what materials
we can find

lady wilson

the cure for anything is salt water:

sweat,

tears

or the sea

isak dinesen

i shut
my eyes
in order
to see

paul gauguin

that love
is all there is,

is all we know of love

those whom true love has held

it
will

go
on

holding

seneca

there is no remedy for love

but to love more

henry david thoreau

nothing
is more
the child of art
than a garden

sir walter scott

who,
being loved,

is poor?

oscar wilde

how fair is a garden

amid the toils and passions

of existence

benjamin disraeli

love many
trust few

always paddle your own canoe

old proverb

you can never get a cup of tea
large enough
or a book long enough
to suit me

cs lewis

friendship
is a
sheltering tree

samuel taylor coleridge

may you have warmth in your igloo,

oil in your lamp,

and peace in your heart

eskimo proverb

let us be grateful to people who make us happy

they are the charming gardeners
who make our souls blossom

marcel proust

hold
tenderly
that
which
you
cherish

bob alberti

hold a true friend with both your hands

nigerian proverb

i am still learning

michelangelo

be silly,

be honest,

be kind

ralph waldo emerson

autumn is a second spring where every leaf is a flower
albert camus

if you have
two loaves
of bread

sell one
and
buy
a hyacinth

old persian saying

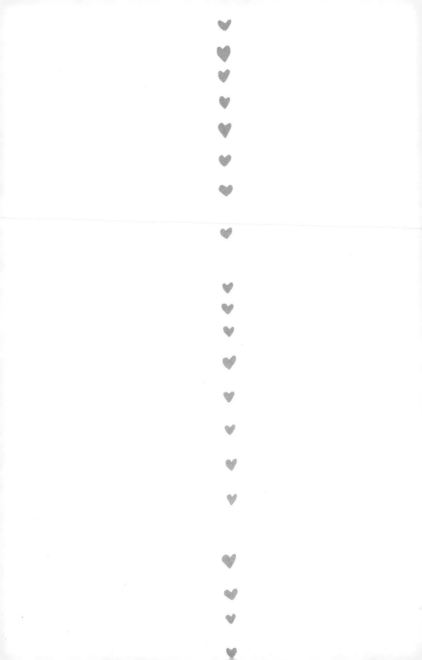

at
one
glance

i love you

with

a thousand hearts

mihri hatun

why,

sometimes

i've believed as many as six impossible things

before breakfast

lewis carroll

a society grows great
when old men plant trees
whose shade
they know
they will never sit in

greek proverb

faith is the substance of things hoped for,

the evidence of things not seen

fill
your
paper

with the breathings of your heart

william wordsworth

constant use

had not worn ragged
the fabric

of their
friendship

dorothy parker

fall seven times
stand up eight

japanese proverb

if you are not too long

i will wait here for you
all my life

oscar wilde

i carry your heart with me
(i carry it in my heart)

♥

ee cummings

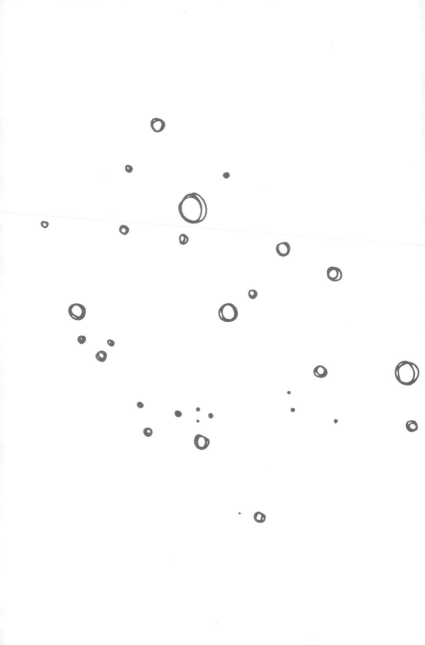

about the author

A poet from childhood, Kylie Johnson has always loved words. Early in her career, she self-published three collections of poetry. Her next two books were published by Murdoch Books, with *count me the stars* (2008) and *a once courageous heart* (2010) both receiving international attention. Kylie has a ceramic gallery and design studio, paper boat press, in Ashgrove, Brisbane. It is here that her signature ceramic quote tags, Christmas ornaments and much-loved poetry vessels are produced.

acknowledgements

I would like to say a few thank-yous to those who have stood by me in this creative life.

Those I trust, there are a quite a few, and those I love, there are many ...

To Alex, my publisher and now friend, for your overwhelming enthusiasm and for your unwavering trust in my vision, I thank you so very much.

My current ceramic work could not be realised without the love and support of my wonderful team of paper boat press girls (past and present) who also happen to be some of my best friends in this big beautiful world: Tiffany, Lisa, Jennifer, Selene, Sarah, Teresa, Danielle, Toni, Anna and Maria. You keep me happy and sane amongst the pressures of the day-to-day running of the studio, gallery and business. I feel so blessed to be surrounded by such amazing women, and to share our lives, the highs and lows, as we work. That, from time to time, we enjoy chocolate and cocktails together while working is just a bonus.

I am also so very grateful to my creative circle of dear *dear* friends who keep me inspired, share their creative lives, and show me even more beauty than I thought possible: Kim, Lincoln, Alischa, Lou, Bridget, Liana, Bec, Maria B, Michelle, Tiel, Clairy, Erin, Iz, Kate, Peter, Linda, Leonard, Katrina, Pia and Kara.

To Jo, Kellie, Judi, Kay, Mel, Nina, Karen, Karen and Karen, Mr and Mrs B, Aunty Rhonnda, and Simon, who have stood by me through it all.

Again, to Sarah, my wing girl, who just knows.

Thank you to my incredibly talented brother, Luke, for everything you are.

To my sister, Tiffany, you bless me with your wisdom, friendship and humour.

To my mum and dad who have never once questioned their belief in my art, my poetry, and my rambling career. For teaching me that being secure in spirit is paramount. For encouraging me to take risks. For teaching me *and* showing me through how they live to be a maker and a doer. And most of all for teaching me how to see, understand and love art, ceramics and words from the moment I was born.

And, finally, thank you to all my followers and collectors who have treasured my work over the years. It is for you I get up and work. I am a maker and a dreamer. With your purchase and love of my work – with this exchange – my art exists in the world and not just in my home.

Your support gives my work its wings.

wisdom and wonder by Kylie Johnson

First published in 2014 as *melancholy and bright* by
University of Queensland Press,
PO Box 6042, St Lucia, Queensland 4067, Australia
This UK edition published in 2016 by Hardie Grant Books

Hardie Grant Books (UK)
5th & 6th Floors
52–54 Southwark Street
London SE1 1UN
www.hardiegrant.co.uk

Hardie Grant Books (Australia)
Ground Floor, Building 1
658 Church Street
Melbourne, VIC 3121
www.hardiegrant.com.au

British Library Cataloguing-in-Publication Data. A catalogue record
for this book is available from the British Library.

ISBN: 978-1-78488-030-9

Cover and text design: Kylie Johnson
Typeset in Georgia by Post Pre-Press Group, Brisbane
Publisher: Kate Pollard
Senior Editor: Kajal Mistry
Editorial Assistant: Hannah Roberts
Pre-Press by P2D

Printed and bound in China by 1010

10 9 8 7 6 5 4 3 2 1